Women Who Win

Cynthia Cooper

Mia Hamm

Martina Hingis

Chamique Holdsclaw

Michelle Kwan

Lisa Leslie

Sheryl Swoopes

Venus & Serena Williams

CHELSEA HOUSE PUBLISHERS

WOMEN WHO WIN

MARTINA HINGIS

Christin Ditchfield

Introduction by
HANNAH STORM

CHELSEA HOUSE PUBLISHERS
Philadelphia

Frontis: *Martina Hingis celebrates her win after defeating Venus Williams for the 1997 U.S. Open women's singles title. That year Martina became the youngest tennis player ever to be ranked No. 1 in the world.*

Produced by
21st Century Publishing and Communications, Inc.
New York, New York
http://www.21cpc.com

CHELSEA HOUSE PUBLISHERS

The Chelsea House World Wide Web address is
http://www.chelseahouse.com

First Printing

1 3 5 7 9 8 6 4 2

Library of Congress Cataloging-in-Publication Data

Ditchfield, Christin.
Martina Hingis / Christin Ditchfield; introduction by Hannah Storm.
p. cm. – (Women who win)
Includes bibliographical references and index.
Summary: Examines the life and career of the only tennis player in history to win the singles and doubles titles in the same Grand Slam event for three consecutive years.
ISBN 0-7910-5797-6 (hc) — ISBN 0-7910-6157-4 (pbk)
1. Hingis, Martina, 1980- —Juvenile literature. 2. Tennis players—Switzerland—Biography—Juvenile literature. 3. Women tennis players—Switzerland—Biography—Juvenile literature. [1. Hingis, Martina, 1980- 2. Tennis players. 3. Women—Biography.] I. Title. II. Series.

GV994.H56 D58 2001
796.342'092—dc21
[B] 00—022841
CIP
AC

Contents

WOMEN WHO WIN

Hannah Storm

NBC Studio Host

You go girl! Women's sports are the hottest thing going right now, with the 1900s ending in a big way. When the U.S. team won the 1999 Women's World Cup, it captured the imagination of all sports fans and served as a great inspiration for young girls everywhere to follow their dreams.

That was just the exclamation point on an explosive decade for women's sports—capped off by the Olympic gold medals for the U.S. women in hockey, softball, and basketball. All the excitement created by the U.S. national basketball team helped to launch the Women's National Basketball Association (WNBA), which began play in 1997. The fans embraced the concept, and for the first time, a successful and stable women's professional basketball league was formed.

I was the first ever play-by-play announcer for the WNBA—a big personal challenge. Broadcasting, just like sports, had some areas with limited opportunities for women. There have traditionally not been many play-by-play opportunities for women in sports television, so I had no experience. To tell you the truth, the challenge I faced was a little scary! Sometimes we are all afraid that we might not be up to a certain task. It is not easy to take risks, but unless we push ourselves we will stagnate and not grow.

Here's what happened to me. I had always wanted to do play-by-play earlier in my career, but I had never gotten the opportunity. Not that I was unhappy—I had been given studio hosting assignments that were unprecedented for a woman and my reputation was well established in the business. I was comfortable in my role . . . plus I had just had my first baby. The last thing I needed to do was suddenly tackle a new skill on national television and risk being criticized (not to mention, very stressed out!). Although I had always wanted to do play-by-play, I turned down the assignment twice, before reluctantly agreeing to give it a try. During my hosting stint of the NBA finals that year, I traveled back and forth to WNBA preseason games to practice play-by-play. I was on 11 flights in 14 days to seven different cities! My head was spinning and it was no surprise that I got sick. On the day of the first broadcast, I had to have shots just so I could go on the air without throwing up. I felt terrible and nervous, but

I survived my first game. I wasn't very good but gradually, week by week, I got better. By the end of the season, the TV reviews of my work were much better—*USA Today* called me "most improved."

During that 1997 season, I witnessed a lot of exciting basketball moments, from the first historic game to the first championship, won by the Houston Comets. The challenge of doing play-by-play was really exciting and I loved interviewing the women athletes and seeing the fans' enthusiasm. Over one million fans came to the games; my favorite sight was seeing young boys wearing the jerseys of female players—pretty cool. And to think I almost missed out on all of that. It reinforced the importance of taking chances and not being afraid of challenges or criticism. When we have an opportunity to follow our dreams, we need to go for it!

Thankfully, there are now more opportunities than ever for women in sports (and other areas, like broadcasting). We thank women, like those in this series, who have persevered despite lack of opportunities—women who have refused to see their limitations. Remember, women's sports has been around a long time. Way back in 396 B.C., Kyniska, a Spartan princess, won an Olympic chariot race. Of course, women weren't allowed to compete, so she was not allowed to collect her prize in person. At the 1996 Olympic games in Atlanta, Georgia, over 35,600 women competed, almost a third more than in the previous Summer Games. More than 20 new women's events have been added for the Sydney, Australia, Olympics in 2000. Women's collegiate sports continues to grow, spurred by the 1972 landmark legislation Title IX, which states that "no person in the United States shall, on the basis of sex, be excluded from participation in, be denied the benefits of, or be subjected to discrimination under any educational program or activity receiving federal financial assistance." This has set the stage for many more scholarships and opportunities for women, and now we have professional leagues as well. No longer do the most talented basketball players in the country have to go to Europe or Asia to earn a living.

The women in this series did not have as many opportunities as you have today. But they were persistent through all obstacles, both on the court and off. I can tell you that Cynthia Cooper is the strongest woman I know. What is it that makes Cynthia and the rest of the women included in this series so special? They are not afraid to share their struggles and their stories with us. Their willingness to show us their emotions, open their hearts, bare their souls, and let us into their lives is what, in my mind, separates them from their male counterparts. So accept this gift of their remarkable stories and be inspired. Because *you*, too, have what it takes to follow your dreams.

1

"I Showed You!"

When 16-year-old tennis pro Martina Hingis arrived in Sydney, Australia, she knew she was ready to win her first Grand Slam title. The Swiss teenager felt confident of a victory. Her mother and coach, Melanie Molitor, wasn't so sure. They had just spent the Christmas holidays visiting family in the Czech Republic. The cold weather had kept Martina from putting in much practice time. Now in January, a month later, she was warming up for the 1997 Australian Open—the first major tournament of the year. Melanie knew that a competitor must be in top physical condition to face the rigors of Grand Slam competition. She doubted that Martina could pull it off. "If you want to win that tournament, you have to work for it," she warned her daughter. "If you're really ready, then show me."

Martina took her mother's words as a challenge. After all, she was used to proving people wrong. When she first became a professional tennis player at age 14, many people shook their heads in disbelief. They insisted that a girl of her age could not possibly handle the intense pressure of competing with adults at an international level. But Martina

---

Martina on her way to victory over Mary Pierce in the 1997 Australian Open. The win marked the first of her three Grand Slam titles in that year.

The beautiful skyline of Sydney, Australia, site of the 1997 Australian Open. There, Martina became the youngest Grand Slam singles champion in 110 years.

didn't listen. Instead, she set out to show the world exactly what she could handle. In her first two years on the tour, she captured three singles titles and two doubles titles—including the 1996 Wimbledon Ladies' Doubles Championship with partner Helena Sukova. She won over $1 million in prize money and set a string of "youngest ever" records. Martina consistently beat Top 10 players, as she moved steadily up the rankings—from No. 87 in 1994, to No. 16 in 1995, to No. 4 in 1996.

Still, some people questioned whether or not Martina would ever be able to achieve true greatness in the sport. It was obvious that she had a lot of talent, but she lacked discipline and maturity. She could hit a stinging backhand down the line, but her second serve needed work. Most of the time, she bubbled over with confidence and enthusiasm. Other times, her temper got the best of her. When she didn't play well or got a bad call from the umpire, she would throw her racquet and stomp around the court like a spoiled child. Her anger and frustration cost her some matches. Tennis journalist and family friend Heinz Mazenauer had followed Martina's tennis career since she was just eight years old. When asked about her potential, he said, "I don't know if she has that killer instinct that top champions have. At this stage, she's the kind of player who plays well when she feels like it, when she is in a good mood. I'm not sure how far that can take a player in today's game." At the 1997 Australian Open, the Swiss teenager was definitely in a good mood—and it took her all the way to the top.

At the National Tennis Centre in Sydney, temperatures soared to over 104 degrees Fahrenheit. Many of the world's best players wilted in the heat. By the end of the first week, six of the top seven women had already been beaten, including Aranxta Sanchez-Vicario, Anke Huber, Lindsay Davenport, and world No. 1 Steffi Graf.

But in spite of the heat and the intense competition, Martina kept her cool. In the two weeks of the tournament, she never even dropped a set. Her closest match came in the fourth round, when Ruxandra Dragomir forced her to a first set tiebreaker. Martina squeaked out an 8-6 win in the tiebreaker and swept the second set 6-1 to win the match. In her quarterfinal match, she fought off eighth-seeded Irina Spirlea 7-5, 6-4. Then, in the semifinals, she blew past American Mary Joe Fernandez 6-1, 6-3.

Between matches, Martina tried to stay calm and relaxed. She went roller-blading along the banks of the Yarra River or in the parking lot behind the tennis complex. She toured the city and took her mother to see the musical production of *Sunset Boulevard.* Martina's off-court adventures made headlines around the world when reporters heard that she had taken a fall while horseback riding. Wasn't it too risky to go riding during a major tournament? What if she had really hurt herself? It could have jeopardized her chances to win. Wasn't her mother worried? Martina quickly dismissed all the media's questions. As for her mother's reaction to the fall? "She was laughing," Martina said. "Everybody was laughing. It wasn't dangerous at all."

The championship match pitted Martina against the hard-hitting French player, Mary Pierce. Pierce had won the Australian Open in 1995. In the three times they had played previously, Pierce had beaten Martina every time. Most recently, at the Canadian Open, Pierce had handed the younger player an embarrassing defeat 6-0, 6-0. But since her Grand Slam win, Mary Pierce's career had been in a slump. Now she was trying to make a comeback.

Martina never gave her the chance. This time, in a match that lasted only 59 minutes, she blasted Pierce 6-2, 6-2. "It was almost scary. I thought, 'It's going so easy.'" Martina later told the press. "She had no winning shot against me today which I couldn't reach. I played almost the perfect match!" Mary Pierce admitted, "Martina has definitely improved since the last time I played her."

As she walked into the locker room after the final match, Martina remembered what her mother had said to her at the start of the tournament. "I showed you!" She told her mother. "Yes," answered Melanie, "and I can't say I'm unhappy about it!"

Martina's victory made history and put her in the record books again. At age 16, she became the youngest player to win a Grand Slam singles title in 110 years! Not since 15-year-old Lottie Dodd won Wimbledon in 1887 had there been a younger champion. Martina herself didn't seem all that excited about the achievement. When the press asked her how it felt to accomplish such an amazing feat, she replied, "It's just another record for me. I mean, I have so many records already." It sounded cocky, but it was true.

Martina's smile says it all as she poses with the Australian Open trophy and a stuffed kangaroo mascot after winning her first Grand Slam title.

At the same tournament, young Martina also captured the Australian Open doubles title with the help of her partner, Natasha Zvereva. They defeated Americans Lindsay Davenport and Lisa Raymond in straight sets 6-2, 6-2. During the trophy presentation, Martina joked that the only reason she hadn't entered the mixed doubles event was that she wanted to give someone else a chance to win. But next year, she said, she would try to win all three events.

When the new world rankings came out after the tournament, Martina had moved up to the No. 2 spot, right behind all-time great Steffi Graf. With a single victory, Martina had proven to the tennis community and the world that she deserved her place among the best players on the professional women's tour. And that was just the beginning.

COREL
WTA
Tacchini

2

Born to Be a Champion

Martina's mother, Melanie Molitor, claims she knew Martina was destined to be a tennis star since she came out of the womb. As a teenager, Melanie herself had been a fairly good tennis player. She grew up in Czechoslovakia, the same country that produced tennis legends Ivan Lendl and Martina Navratilova. Melanie felt a tremendous respect and admiration for Navratilova, who would go on to become one of the greatest female players of all time. On at least one occasion, Melanie had the privilege of practicing with Navratilova. It made a big impression on the junior player. Melanie's ranking peaked at No. 20 in the nation's junior levels. She was good, but not good enough to make it on the professional tennis tour.

Eventually, Melanie Molitor met and married a tennis coach named Karol Hingis. On September 30, 1980, Melanie gave birth to a baby girl. She named her Martina, after her countrywoman, Martina Navratilova. With two parents who loved tennis, it was only natural that little Martina would learn to love it, too. Melanie and Karol gave the little girl her first racquet when she was just two years old. It was an

Martina hugs her mother and coach, Melanie Molitor. Determined to make her daughter a tennis star, Melanie trained and guided Martina all the way to the top of the tennis world. She also named her daughter after her idol, tennis legend Martina Navratilova.

adult-sized racquet, but the handle had been shaved down until it was thin enough for Martina to get her tiny hand around it.

From the beginning, Melanie was determined to make her daughter a tennis champion. She did everything she could to encourage Martina to play. Together, they tossed a tennis ball back and forth in the house. Firmly grasping her special racquet, Martina would try to hit the ball back to her mother. They practiced for about 20 minutes each day.

When she was three years old, Martina began to play regularly at the tennis club where her father worked. "I grew up on tennis courts, I was there day and night," Martina remembers. "When I was very young, I would spend 16 hours a day at the club, though not always playing tennis. I would play other games like the other kids, but I would play doubles with the guys. I was a wall. If the ball was near me, I brought it back. . . . I . . . was playing with kids three or four years older and my only chance was to not be the worst player on the court."

Tennis is not an easy game for a child to play. A sportswriter once asked Martina how she could have seen over the top of the net. Martina explained that, at first, she *couldn't*. "You can see a little bit *through* the net," she said. "But I only saw the ball when it was coming at me!"

Martina entered her first tournament at age four. The competition was open to players up to nine years old. "I lost very badly," Martina admits. "I knew where to stand and how to play a little bit, but I couldn't make it then. I lost 12-0—but I had my chances in every game!"

Martina's parents divorced during that same year. A few years later, her mother married a

As a child, Martina moved with her mother to Switzerland. She came to love the beautiful lakes and mountains and her new, outdoor lifestyle there.

Swiss businessman, Andreas Zogg, and mother and daughter moved to Switzerland. Martina later described the move as one of the most difficult times in her life. She had to learn a new language, make new friends, and adjust to life in a different country. But the athletic, outdoor lifestyle of the Swiss people appealed to Martina. In addition to tennis, she enjoyed swimming, skiing, boxing, basketball, soccer, and aerobics. She spent hours riding her horse in the mountains and caring for her dog, a German Shepherd named Zorro.

As Martina grew, so did her skills. At nine years old, she started to compete in international tournaments. Because of her skill level, she played in an age bracket that included 14-year-olds. At age 10, Martina began to win. The next year, the young player reached some major milestones. She won a very prestigious junior tournament—the European Championships. She was also beginning to regularly outplay her mother in their practice games. It actually embarrassed Martina a little. "As soon as I beat her, I didn't want to play her. I only wanted to play left-handed against her," she says.

Melanie Molitor didn't mind at all. She was thrilled to see her daughter develop her skills so quickly. She continued to coach Martina herself, but she found new practice partners to help challenge her talented little girl. She also got advice from tennis experts on the best coaching techniques. While the ambitious mother took Martina's training very seriously, she was careful not to push her daughter too hard. She encouraged Martina to develop other interests and hobbies outside of tennis.

On the tennis court, Martina's game continued to improve. In 1993 she took on the international junior tennis circuit. At 12, Martina became the youngest player ever to win a Grand Slam junior title—the French Open. The previous record-holder had been teen sensation Jennifer Capriati. A month later, Martina reached the semifinals in both the singles and doubles competitions at the junior Wimbledon event. Many in the tennis community sat up and took notice of the promising young player. World-famous coach Nick Bolletieri was one of those who watched her play. Bolletieri had worked with tennis stars such as Andre Agassi, Monica Seles, Jim Courier, Mary Pierce, and Boris Becker. He recognized the youngster's talent right away: "She was awful sloppy. No serve. But once she played the points, she knew exactly what to do with the ball. She had an animal instinct for the game, an exceptionally strong mentality. . . . Talents like this happen once or twice in a lifetime. . . . She's just a born winner!"

Later that year, Martina competed in several satellite tournaments (tennis's version of the minor leagues). Just after her 13th birthday, she captured her first professional title at the International Tennis Federation (ITF) Women's Circuit event in Langenthal, Switzerland. Barely a teenager, Martina remained eligible to participate in junior tournaments. Her 1994 season was phenomenal.

As the defending junior champion, Martina repeated her success in Paris, capturing her second French Open junior singles title. She walked away with the junior doubles trophy, too. At 13 years, 276 days old, Martina Hingis became the youngest Wimbledon junior singles champion ever. She capped off a fantastic year by reaching the finals of the junior U.S. Open. The ITF named her Junior of the Year.

As the best junior player in the world, Martina had racked up impressive victories, set amazing records, and reached the top of the amateur tennis world. What more could she hope to accomplish? Could it possibly be time to turn pro?

Sergio Tacchini

3

"Proceed With Caution"

Martina Hingis faced a difficult decision. Already the top junior player in the world, she didn't have anything left to accomplish in amateur tennis. Could she really be ready to join the professional women's tour at age 14?

If she turned pro now, she wouldn't be the youngest player ever to do so. Jennifer Capriati held that record when she took the plunge into the adult world of professional tennis at 13 years old. Like Martina, Capriati had showed incredible talent and potential from an early age. Overnight she became a "media darling." Everything she said or did made front-page news. Her bubbly personality and irrepressible giggle won the hearts of people everywhere. Her agents signed her to endorsement contracts worth millions of dollars. She agreed to advertise everything from shoes to clothes to cosmetics, before she had even won her first professional match. At first it seemed like a fairy-tale dream come true. Capriati reached the finals of the first tournament she entered and, within a year of joining the pro tour, she ranked among the Top 10 women players in the world. She seemed destined for tennis superstardom.

Martina swings during a 1995 tournament in Philadelphia. At 13, she was named ITF Junior of the Year and faced the decision whether to turn pro at age 14.

But the dream quickly turned into a nightmare. Capriati carried the weight of the world on her young shoulders. She tried to live up to all the expectations and wanted to please her parents, her agents, and her fans. It was enormous pressure for such a young girl. The constant attention from the news media only added to her stress. In the middle of it all, she had to compete at the highest levels against some of the best athletes in the world. It was just too much. Capriati's life began to unravel. She couldn't maintain the intensity she needed on the court. She lost some big matches and her confidence suffered. She quickly went from being a bubbly little girl to an angry, sullen teenager. The newspaper headlines started to focus on her career slump, her family problems, and her experimentation with drugs and alcohol.

Capriati's breakdown left everyone searching for answers and pointing fingers. People were especially critical of the media, which had constantly invaded her privacy, forcing her to live her life on display for all the world to see. What about Capriati's parents? Did they push their daughter too hard in hopes of financial gain? Or was it the fault of the Women's Tennis Association (WTA) for allowing such a young girl to compete in the first place?

The tennis community had experienced all of this before. Andrea Jaeger and Tracy Austin were both teenage tennis stars whose careers were cut short by injury and burnout. The constant physical, emotional, and mental strain had taken its toll on them. Yet in spite of the obvious dangers, younger and younger players pushed their way into the professional ranks, lured by the promise of stardom and

Jennifer Capriati, became a professional tennis player at 13. Capriati's difficulties as a child star and her eventual breakdown led the WTA to try to protect young tennis hopefuls by adopting age restrictions for turning pro.

the potential millions of dollars to be made in prize money and endorsements.

After Jennifer Capriati, everyone agreed that something had to change. Something had to be done to protect the next generation of tennis stars from destroying themselves before they had a chance to live up to their potential. The WTA formed an Age Eligibility Commission and Advisory Panel. The panel consisted of doctors, sports psychologists, sociologists, and athletic trainers who came together to make recommendations and suggest possible solutions. As a result, the WTA adopted new rules that set age restrictions for players turning pro and competing in tour events.

Under the new rules, girls under age 15 could only play a handful of minor tournaments and would not be allowed to compete on the regular tour. A 15-year-old could join the regular tour and play 8 tournaments a year, a 16-year-old could play 10, and a 17-year-old could compete in 13 events. At age 18, all age restrictions would be lifted and a player could then compete in an unlimited number of tournaments.

The WTA also created the Player Development Program. This program offered young players special classes on nutrition and fitness, access to career counseling, and free medical advice. Each player under 18 would now be assigned a mentor—a veteran player who would offer guidance and encouragement as needed.

The new rules received mixed reviews from the rest of the tennis community. Some thought the Player Development Program and the age restrictions were a step in the right direction, though long overdue. Others felt that the new rules didn't go far enough.

Right in the middle of all these changes, Martina Hingis announced her decision to turn pro. Like Capriati, Martina already had an agent. She had endorsement contracts with Sergio Tacchini clothing, Opel cars, and Yonex racquets. Martina and her mother, Melanie, both felt that she was ready to take on the challenges of the professional tour. Martina's announcement sparked more controversy and debate. The board members of the WTA found themselves in an awkward position. They had just made rules that would prevent the brightest new player from being able to compete. There were rumors that Martina and a hot young American player, Venus Williams, might sue the tour if they were not allowed to play. To avoid any potential legal problems and afraid of losing the media coverage and positive publicity that Martina and Williams would bring, the WTA quietly allowed both girls to turn pro before the new rules went into effect.

To Martina and her mother, it was a relief. They could move forward with Martina's career as they planned. But many people openly opposed the WTA's decision. Tennis legend Martina Navratilova, Martina's namesake, was asked if she thought the young player should be allowed to turn pro. "I don't," she answered. "But who am I?"

Tennis historian and TV commentator Bud Collins called Martina "a revelation, a champion-to-be. . . . [S]he is a true prodigy, a delight to behold, an interesting and entertaining shot-maker." At the same time, he also said that he remained opposed to anyone turning pro before age 18. "Tennis has fostered too many teenage wrecks."

Journalists, coaches, players, and experts all weighed in with their own opinions. Some described Melanie Molitor as a greedy, pushy, demanding parent who would destroy her daughter with her ambition for tennis glory. Others said Melanie Molitor was well-meaning, but misguided. They believed she should not allow her daughter to turn pro.

Regardless of the criticism, mother and daughter could not be swayed. They believed in their hearts that the time was right. Melanie explained: "We've worked 10 years for this. It's a natural development." Martina shrugged off questions and comments about Jennifer Capriati's struggles. "She's just one person,"

Melanie Molitor supervises Martina's training. Martina says that her mother is not only her coach but also her best friend, who lends her support whenever it is needed.

Martina said. "There are a thousand girls in the rankings."

On October 4, 1994, Martina Hingis stepped onto the court in Zurich, Switzerland, for her first match as a professional tennis player. She faced an experienced opponent, 29-year-old American Patty Fendick, who was ranked among the Top 50 players in the world. Over 170 members of the press gathered to cover the match. In spite of the incredible pressure, Martina showed no trace of nervousness or anxiety. She did not appear to be aware of all the media hype, and easily defeated the veteran player in straight sets 6-4, 6-3. In her post-match interview, Martina was casual and relaxed. When asked how she felt about winning her first professional match, she responded, "I'm not that surprised. I've beaten better players."

In her next match, Martina was defeated by the No. 5-ranked player, Mary Pierce of France. Her first shot at a professional title ended in the second round. The performance may not have been spectacular, but it was certainly respectable. It seemed she was well on her way.

Still, some people remained unconvinced that Martina and her mother had made the right decision. *Sports Illustrated* devoted a feature article to Martina's debut entitled "Proceed With Caution." Writer Sally Jenkins observed that the young player had "elegant groundstrokes, a champion's two-handed backhand, a sound grasp of strategy and a composure far beyond her years." But Jenkins then went on to discuss the need for the new age limits and the WTA's controversial decision to allow Martina to compete. The writer expressed grave doubts as to whether Martina would be able to withstand the pressures of life on the pro tour.

Jenkins concluded, "[T]he latest child prodigy has arrived. There is nothing to be done about it but admire Hingis's immense talent and hope that this story, against the odds, has a happy ending." She didn't sound very optimistic.

Martina paid no attention to the debate or the doubts. She approached the 1995 season, her first full year on the pro tour, with excitement and enthusiasm. In January, Martina competed in her first adult Grand Slam event—the Australian Open. There are four Grand Slam tournaments each year: Wimbledon, the Australian Open, French Open, and U.S. Open. These tournaments are the largest, most prestigious tennis competitions in the world. They are called "Grand Slam" events because a player who wins all four of the tournaments in the same year is said to have won a "Grand Slam."

Martina had won several junior Grand Slam titles, but this time she would be competing against adults. In the first round, at age 14 years and four months, Martina Hingis became the youngest female player in the Open Era to win a singles match at the Australian Open. She reached the second round at the Australian and French Opens but lost in the first round at Wimbledon. Her best Grand Slam results came at the U.S. Open, where she reached the fourth round.

She didn't win any tournament titles in her first season, but she competed well and gained some much-needed experience. In Hamburg, Germany, Martina defeated two Top 10 players, Jana Novotna of the Czech Republic and Anke Huber, to reach her first professional tournament final. There she lost a tough match to Conchita Martinez of Spain.

Actually, Martina had quite a good year. She surprised even herself by skyrocketing to No. 16 in the world rankings. "I never really thought I would be able to move up so quickly this year," she said. "It went so fast, it was unexpected and incredible."

The women's tour honored Martina with the Most Impressive Newcomer Award, and *Tennis* magazine named her Rookie of the Year. *Tennis* noted that, although she was named for Navratilova, Martina Hingis played a lot more like Navratilova's greatest rival, Chris Evert. Both Evert and Martina played an intelligent, conservative, baseline game. Like Evert, Martina had incredible accuracy with her groundstrokes and used strategy—not strength—to defeat her opponents. Both women had reputations for being calm and composed. They played with confidence under pressure. A TV commentator once said that Martina was so cool on the court, she sweated drops of ice water.

With time and experience, Martina's game would only continue to improve. She had just one weakness—her serve. But mom and coach Melanie Molitor said that the weak serve was all a part of the plan. "I don't want Martina overworking her muscles with weights and exercises when she is so young and her body is still developing. As she gets stronger physically, she will be able to do more strengthening exercises and hit the ball harder. But it's not important now, because that will come soon enough."

After a full year on the tour, Martina would be watched even more closely by the tennis world. They were waiting to see if she would crack under the pressure that had so quickly destroyed other young players. But Martina was still standing strong.

IZEN
ATCH TIME

4

"Doing Pretty Good for My Age"

For Martina Hingis, the 1996 tennis season was crucial. The young player needed to show the world that she belonged on the professional women's tour. She had done well in her rookie year. Would she continue to grow and develop as a player? Or would she fall apart like so many other tennis teens?

The world didn't have to wait long for an answer. In January, Martina returned to Sydney, Australia, to set yet another record. She fought past Brenda Schultz-McCarthy in the fourth round to become the youngest player ever to reach the quarterfinals at the Australian Open.

With the help of her mother, Martina worked hard to improve her game. She practiced forehands and backhands, as well as volleys and serves. She began to develop her own style of play. All the hard work paid off, and the results soon showed.

In May, Martina competed at the Italian Open in Rome. She got through to the quarterfinals, where she faced the No. 1 player in the world, Steffi Graf. Martina's game was on; her shot selection was brilliant. She made the former

---

Martina returns the ball to Steffi Graf during the women's semifinals singles match at the 1996 U.S. Open. Only 15 years old, Martina reached the semifinals in the singles, doubles, and mixed doubles events.

champion look sluggish and disoriented on the court. In a stunning upset, the Swiss teenager defeated Graf in three sets 2-6, 6-2, 6-3.

"I've got to get myself in better shape," Graf said after the match. "I had no confidence in any of my strokes. I had no rhythm." It may have been a disappointing loss for Steffi, but for Martina it was a thrilling victory. "It is a great chance to play against No. 1—and I took it!" Martina said. "She beat me bad the other two times we played. This was the match of my life!"

Martina had earned her first big win over a top-ranked player. But she couldn't celebrate for long. She had another match to play. In the semifinals, Martina continued her incredible run at the clay-court tournament. She handily defeated the No. 7-ranked player, Irina Spirlea. With that victory, Martina became the youngest Italian Open finalist since Tracy Austin in 1979.

Truthfully, Martina had expected to lose in the early rounds. She planned to spend the weekend shopping or sightseeing in Rome before heading off to the next event. Instead, Martina found herself playing for the championship. Unfortunately she ran out of steam in the final match. Defending champion Conchita Martinez beat the young player in straight sets.

"It wasn't my backhands and forehands," Martina later explained to the press. "My head was the biggest problem. I just couldn't keep concentration. Probably everything that has happened this week was a little too much. I was already in the final and I was happy with that."

Martina had good reason to be pleased with her performance. As one newspaper headline put it, "Conchita Martinez captures fourth straight Italian Open, but Martina Hingis is the talk of Rome!"

For the first time, Martina received media coverage for her success and accomplishments rather than for her controversial decision to turn pro. Reporters gave her nicknames like "The Can't Miss Swiss" and "Heidi of the Hardcourts." *Tennis* magazine ran an article entitled "Hingis's High-Powered Backhand." They showed photos of the 15-year-old's backhand shot as an example for all aspiring tennis players to imitate. The article quoted tennis great Tony Trabert: "Martina Hingis is one of the most exciting young players on the women's tour. Not only does she possess a world of talent, but also she's mechanically sound and displays unusual self-confidence and on-court poise. . . . I think she's destined to be one of the top players—maybe the best player—in women's tennis."

Although things were going extremely well for her, Martina still faced some frustrations. The WTA Tour had made a special exception to its new rules in order to allow Martina to turn pro. But they did place some restrictions on her play.

"The rule that limits the tournaments I can play still affects my ranking," Martina complained. "It is hard to break into the Top 10 when you are restricted by how much you can play. There have to be rules, but I also know that until I turn sixteen and can play an unlimited schedule, my ranking will not be as good as it can be."

Martina still found herself answering a lot of questions from reporters about the challenges of being a professional athlete at her age. They kept hinting that her schedule was too grueling, that it was too much pressure and too much work for someone her age.

"I only practice tennis for about one and a

half hours a day," explained Martina, sometimes impatiently. "[That's] less time than I usually spend riding my horse, Montana. I do other sports, like aerobics and basketball and soccer, and sometimes I go running with my dog. It's true that I'm not in school like other kids my age, but I don't feel I am missing something there. I have many friends on the tour."

She added, "People always ask me if I miss normal life, and my answer is always the same: I feel I *have* a normal life, even if it's not the same life as other kids. It is maybe even better than a normal life, because my life actually is like always holidays. That's because I like tennis."

What about the media hype? Didn't the constant glare of the spotlight bother her? "The attention has not affected me at all. It does not change a thing," Martina insisted. "There is always a lot of media and publicity to do at tournaments, but that's part of my job. It only lasts while I'm at tournaments. Then I can go home and ride my horse in the Swiss mountains and get away from it all. I can relax and do what I want."

Some people accused Melanie Molitor of being pushy or overbearing, but Martina was quick to defend her mom. "I love traveling with my mother . . . and having her as my coach," she said. "In fact, she's everything to me: coach, mother, and best friend. She always has my best interests at heart and she's always there to support me. Like all families, we argue sometimes but we always find a compromise. She has sacrificed a lot for me, and I'm glad that we can share this success together."

Martina's success at the Grand Slams continued in 1996. She reached the third round at the French Open and the fourth round at

Martina and Helena Sukova (left), share the ladies doubles trophy at the 1996 Wimbledon. With their victory, Martina entered the record books as the youngest Wimbledon winner in over 100 years.

Wimbledon. At Wimbledon she won her first professional doubles title with her partner Helena Sukova. The doubles victory made Martina the youngest Wimbledon winner since Lottie Dodd in 1887, and the first Swiss woman ever to win a Wimbledon crown.

In August, Martina headed to the U.S. Open, determined to give an all-out effort. She played in singles, doubles, and mixed doubles competition. Incredibly, she reached the semifinals in all three events. In the singles semifinals, Martina ran into Steffi Graf once again. This time, Graf was ready for her, and Martina did not have the energy to pull off an upset. She realized that she had taken on more than she could handle. "Playing all three events was a lot," she admitted. "But I never thought that I would get so far in all of them." Graf defeated Martina in straight sets.

Steffi Graf (left) congratulates Martina after being defeated by her at the 1996 Italian Open. Later that year, Graf beat Martina in a difficult match in New York but praised Martina's developing skills on the court.

In a post-match interview, Graf commented on the improvement in Martina's game: "The way she's been playing, you can't really look at her as a 15-year-old!" she said.

Martina could be proud of her effort and the three semifinal results. Before they left New York, Martina and her mother took a few days off. They went to see the Broadway production of *Les Misérables*, and Martina visited the horses at the Belmont race track.

However, the 1996 season wasn't over yet. There were still more tournaments to play, and the competition would keep getting tougher. One of Martina's friends, tennis teen Iva Majoli explained, "I think now everybody expects Martina to win more, and in her own head she is now a little older, a little more conscious of where she should be or wants to be, in the rankings. At the same time, she has been on the tour long enough so that the other girls have played her and talked about her and figured out what they want to try to do against her [on the court]. So she has more pressure now. But if she feels this pressure, she doesn't show it."

Martina once told a reporter, "I want to be number one in the world and I think I can. I've seen the competition, and I'm not afraid. Sometimes I have a bad day and make too many errors. But as I get older, I don't think there will be as many bad days."

She was right. In October, just a week after her 16th birthday, Martina Hingis cracked the Top 10 in the world rankings. She became the third youngest player to do so, after Andrea Jaeger and Jennifer Capriati. Two weeks later, Martina captured her first WTA Tour singles title—the Porsche Grand Prix in Filderstadt, Germany. On the way to the title, she beat three Top-10 players: No. 2 Aranxta Sanchez-Vicario, No. 5 Anke Huber, and No. 6 Lindsay Davenport. Along with the trophy, Martina received a brand new Porsche. Reporters teased her that it would be two more years before she was old enough to drive it. (In Europe the legal driving age is 18.)

Martina's second professional title came within a month of her first. In Oakland, California, Martina shocked the No. 2 player in the world, Monica Seles, 6-2, 6-0 to win the championship match. The victory had special significance for Martina:

"[W]hen I was little I always used to watch Monica Seles. She was my idol," Martina said. "She was playing in a big tournament in Europe and I got her autograph [before she went off in a helicopter]. I was so excited to see her in person. And then six months ago, I was playing her in a tournament. . . . To play Monica for the first time and win . . . wow!"

The victory boosted Martina to her highest ranking yet—No. 6—in the world. It also set another record: Martina Hingis had become the youngest player (male or female) to win more than $1 million in prize money.

Martina's ranking and results through the year qualified her to play in the special season-ending Chase Championships at New York's Madison Square Garden. She made the most of the opportunity. Martina fought her way to the final match, where her opponent was none other than Steffi Graf.

Both women desperately wanted to win the Championships. Graf had been battling back from injuries and hoped to end the year on a positive note. Martina wanted a major title to help prove that she belonged among the best in the world. In most women's tournaments, players must win two out of three sets. But in the Chase Championships, a player must win three out of five sets.

This year, the final turned out to be an epic battle. Martina and Graf fought for every point, every game, every set. Graf took the first set 6-3, but Martina battled back to take the second set 6-4. Graf swept to the lead again in the third set 6-0. Martina hung on and managed to win the fourth set 6-4. But by the fifth set, both players were struggling with new opponents: injury and fatigue. Between games, Graf iced down her muscles and taped up previous injuries. Martina began cramping uncontrollably. At one point, she hurt so badly that she had to lie down on the court. The umpire called for a physical trainer to assess her condition. After an injury time-out, Martina bravely returned to finish out the match. But the older, more experienced player prevailed. Graf won the fifth set 6-0.

The Swiss teenager couldn't help feeling disappointed. "Somehow I wanted to cry," she said. "You make a fifth set against Steffi and then you're really not able to force her anymore, because you don't have the power in yourself. Steffi had a great tournament and she's a big player and she can handle it better than I do."

Graf was pleased with her win, but she had nothing but praise for her young rival: "She can hit incredible angles and she probably has the best down-the-line shots of anybody. You don't see many players doing what she is doing with her strokes. She's got a good view of the court and a good sense out there. The way she is playing, she is definitely the one to look out for!"

The next day, the final rankings came out. Martina had jumped up two more notches to No. 4 in the world. She received the WTA award for Most Improved Player of the Year. Earlier in the year Martina had talked about her career with veteran tennis writer Peter Bodo. "I knew always that I would be a tennis player, but I never felt pushed to be one, and I never worried about how good I could become," she had said. "I think I'm doing pretty good for my age."

Pretty good? After the 1996 season, the tennis world had to admit that Martina was doing great! But they hadn't seen anything yet.

5

PLAYER OF THE YEAR

As the 1997 season began, a reporter asked 16-year-old Martina Hingis how she had changed in her two years on the tour. "[N]ow I am much stronger mentally and physically," Martina replied. "I realized that if I wanted to compete against the bigger girls I had to improve my fitness and quickness. I would get tired sometimes and did not catch up with their power when I played the top girls. But I was never afraid. I just had to learn mentally that I could beat anyone. Once I won the Filderstadt tournament this past year, I got over that and now know I can beat anyone."

To improve her strength and fitness, Martina added weight lifting to her workouts three times a week. She also put more effort into her practices. Martina has often admitted that laziness is one of her biggest problems. She simply doesn't like to practice. It was her desire to avoid boring practice sessions that led her to compete in doubles events on the tour.

"Playing doubles is a lot more fun than practicing," she explains. "I still have to think and work out there, but it is

Martina jumps for joy after defeating Monica Seles in the semifinals of the 1997 French Open. Years before, Martina had been excited just to get Seles's autograph.

fun. It helps my net game and keeps me playing aggressively. And I also don't have to practice as much!"

To begin the new season, Martina headed to Sydney, Australia, once again. She reached the finals of her first tournament, a warm-up event scheduled just before the Australian Open. Martina would play Jennifer Capriati for the title. Capriati had taken several years away from tennis to resolve her personal problems. Now at age 21, the former teen tennis star was attempting a comeback. She fought hard, but Martina walked away with her third WTA Tour title. The year was off to a great start.

By now, setting records at the Australian Open had become a tradition for Martina. This year she went all the way, becoming the youngest player ever to win the Australian Open title. Amazingly, she did it without dropping a single set. She also won the doubles championship with her partner, Natasha Zvereva. The last woman to win both the singles and doubles during the same year was Martina Navratilova in 1985. This first Grand Slam victory thrilled Martina and her mother. But Martina broke something beside the tournament records—she broke her New Year's resolution. "I had a goal this year not to have a [racquet abuse warning], but that ended during just the second match of the year," Martina laughed.

It was true that Martina kept calm under pressure; she didn't get nervous or uptight on the court. However, she did frequently lose her temper when frustrated. After missing a shot or making a mistake, she often banged her racquet on the court in disgust. But Martina made no apologies for her emotions: "I show the difference in how I feel if I am winning or if I am losing,"

Martina shows her emotions on the court. She is sometimes warned for throwing her racquet but says that anger is just a natural part of her character.

she said. "This is part of my character and I wouldn't even think about changing it. If I'm happy, I smile and laugh. If I'm angry or frustrated, I throw my racquet. I shouldn't do that, I know. But I can't help it."

After the Australian Open, Martina competed in the Pan Pacific Open in Japan. She was scheduled to play Steffi Graf in the tournament final. But the veteran player suffered another injury and had to withdraw from the match. Martina won the tournament by default.

Two weeks later, Martina received another singles trophy, this time at the Open Gaz de France. She also won the doubles event with her partner, Jana Novotna. The victory in France made Martina the first woman to win three consecutive tournaments on three different continents (Australia, Asia, and Europe). It also made her the No. 2 player in the world.

As she competed in the Lipton Championships in Key Biscayne, Florida, in March, Martina's game got better and better. She played almost flawless tennis. With Steffi Graf off the tour due to injury, Martina was now the highest-ranked player at the tournament. She blew past every competitor in her path. In the championship match, Martina defeated Monica Seles 6-2, 6-1. The entire match lasted less than 45 minutes.

In her post-match press conference, reporters pointed out that Martina had a terrific winning streak going. So far this year, she was undefeated. They asked Martina if she thought she could keep it up. A little carelessly, she replied, "Why should I be worried about the future when everything is perfect? I don't care about the future. Once you've made it, you know you can do it again."

On March 31, 1997, at 16 years, six months, and one day, Martina Hingis became the youngest player ever to reach No. 1 in the world rankings. In her interviews, Martina bubbled over with joy and excitement. "It's a great feeling to be No. 1 and accomplish that. . . . I feel so good about my game and I am having more fun with my tennis than I ever have had in my life." Someone asked Martina if she considered herself unbeatable. "You can say that I'm unbeatable right now, " she giggled, "because I am!"

One week after the Lipton Championships, Martina competed at the Family Circle Cup in Hilton Head, South Carolina. In a rematch of the Lipton final, Martina and Seles took to the court again. This time, Seles put up a tremendous fight. But the end result was the same: Martina won 3-6, 6-3, 7-6. That week she added two more titles—one singles and one doubles—to her collection. The Family Circle Cup was her sixth professional singles title of the year. She had won 37 straight matches.

The No. 1 player in the world packed up and headed home for a well-deserved break. At home in Switzerland, Martina sustained an injury. While riding a friend's horse near her home in Trubbach, Martina took a bad fall. At first it didn't seem to be too big a deal. By the next day, Martina felt pain and swelling in her left knee. A visit to the doctor revealed that she had torn a ligament. It wasn't a bad tear, but it would require an operation. "Having surgery wasn't any fun," Martina said later. "[A]nd I'm just glad I didn't do any major damage."

Martina had to withdraw from tournaments in Germany and Italy. It would be seven weeks before she rejoined the tour. Many thought Martina's winning streak had been ruined and she had lost her momentum. She couldn't possibly return to the game and pick up where she left off. Or could she?

Through hard work in physical therapy, Martina managed to make it back in time to compete in the French Open. She had no warm-up tournaments and no practice. Many people expected her to lose in the first round. Martina didn't worry about what other people thought. She battled past the newest teen sensation, Anna Kournikova, her doubles partner, Aranxta Sanchez-Vicario, and former champion Monica Seles. But unlike the Australian Open, where she never lost a set, this time Martina's matches were tougher. Three out of her seven matches went to three sets. Everyone had to agree that she did extremely well to reach the final in her first tournament back. Unfortunately, the effort had taken too much out of her. Martina didn't do very well in the final. She missed a lot of shots and made some bad errors. In frustration, she threw her racquet. Some of the spectators booed her. Iva Majoli won the match in straight sets.

It was Martina's first loss of the year, and she took it very hard. However, Martina herself once said, "[T]ennis is not like the Olympic Games, in which you have one chance for happiness every four years. There is a new chance in tennis every week."

Martina's next chance came at Wimbledon, the third Grand Slam event of the year. She badly wanted to erase the memory of her loss in France. As the No. 1 player in the world, Martina went into the tournament with a lot at stake. "There is a lot of pressure that comes with being number one, because I don't want to lose to anyone ranked below me and now *everyone* is ranked below me. Everyone wants to play me now, and they sure want to beat me. It's the same feeling I had when I wasn't on top and wanted to beat the top players, so I'm familiar with it. Yet I've prepared for this moment my whole life."

There were several factors working against Martina at Wimbledon. Her humiliating loss to Majoli at the French Open had affected her confidence. She chose not to play any warm-up events in between the French Open and Wimbledon. Since the two tournaments are played on completely different surfaces (the Open on clay and Wimbledon on grass), they require different preparation and strategy. Martina, having grown up playing on clay, has said, "I hate grass, because you have to think differently." She didn't like to have to change or adjust her game for this particular surface. In spite of the obstacles in her path, Martina found her way through the top half of the draw. She sent every one of her opponents packing in straight sets.

During her post-match press conferences, Martina seemed happy, confident, and eager to play. As always, she spoke her mind freely, never hesitating to say exactly what she thought. When reporters mentioned Steffi Graf's absence due to injury and surgery, Martina responded, "If she's going to come back, for sure it's not going to be the same Steffi as she was. Her career is almost over." When asked about the rivalry between herself and the young Russian star Anna Kournikova, Martina answered, "I don't think it's such a big rivalry. I've always been better, and I always beat her."

In the final, Martina would meet the previous year's runner-up, Jana Novotna. Novotna had a reputation for being a superb grass-court player, but Martina wasn't afraid to take her on. "Jana can play very good tennis, but sometimes she just can't win."

In the first set, Novotna played extremely well. She hit some fantastic shots. And regardless of what she had said before, Martina actually looked a little nervous. She couldn't find her rhythm on the court. Novotna won the first set easily 6-2. In the second set, Martina recovered her poise. She began to mix up her shots and control the rhythm of the match. Her passing shots were perfect; she hit sizzling backhand winners down the line. Nothing Novotna tried could stop her. Martina won the next two sets 6-3, 6-3.

In that moment, Martina Hingis became the

youngest player in the Open Era to win the Wimbledon singles title. "I was there, the Wimbledon champion, standing on Centre Court," she said. "No one can take that from me. I will remember that all my life." Sports journalist Steve Flink wrote, "Martina Hingis demonstrated beyond the shade of a doubt that she is the greatest 16-year-old female competitor the game has yet witnessed."

"She's the one!" said tennis legend Billie Jean King. "I like her cockiness and self-belief. She's not a passive woman. She's saying, 'I'm here, and I'm really good, and I like being here. Watch me!' We've felt for two or three years that she's the best in the world."

The best player in the world was on a roll once again. In her next tournament at Stanford, California, Martina won both the singles and doubles trophies. The results were the same when she competed at the Toshiba Tennis Classic in San Diego. Martina beat Seles for the singles title and went on to win the doubles with her new partner, Aranxta Sanchez-Vicario.

By the end of August, Martina had won a total of nine singles titles—two of them Grand Slams—and five doubles titles. She had solidified her grip on the No. 1 ranking. No one could stop talking about her incredible run. After two weeks of rest and relaxation, Martina arrived in New York for the U.S. Open, ready to take on the world once again.

Just as she did at the Australian Open and at Wimbledon, Martina moved almost effortlessly through the draw. She barely broke a sweat as she dismissed the other players in straight sets. The championship match pitted Martina against the up-and-coming tennis teen, American Venus Williams. Although Williams had turned pro in

Tennis legend Billie Jean King on the cover of Tennis *magazine. King made history in 1973 when she defeated Bobby Riggs, a former Wimbledon champion in a match called "Battle of the Sexes," which drew a TV audience of some 40 million viewers worldwide. King has praised Martina's self-confidence, saying, "She's the best in the world."*

1994, the same year as Martina, she had followed her own path on the tour. For several years, Williams played only a handful of events. Now 17, she had never won a tour title, and this was the first year she was competing in the Grand Slams.

Reaching the final was a major breakthrough for Williams. She became the hot new story. Reporters couldn't get enough of this promising young star who might have the talent to upstage the best players in the world. Momentarily they seemed to forget that Martina—tour veteran,

Martina delights photographers with her smile after becoming the new 1997 Wimbledon women's singles champion. By the end of the 1997 season, Martina had won 12 singles and 8 doubles titles.

winner of two Grand Slams, and the No. 1 player in the world—was actually the younger of the two girls. The all-teen final earned a lot of media attention, but the match didn't live up to the hype. The more experienced player won. Martina soundly defeated Williams 6-0, 6-4.

Prior to the final match, the relationship between Williams and Martina had not always been friendly. Like Martina, Williams had plenty of self-confidence. She dismissed the idea of a future tennis rivalry with Martina by saying that she and her younger sister Serena would be the ones ruling the world rankings in the future. When asked to comment on Williams's predictions, Martina laughed. She quickly pointed out that Venus didn't have the results to back up the big talk. After the U.S. Open final, however, both young women were gracious and complimentary of one another.

"I give Venus credit," said the new U.S. Open champ. "She has improved since I played her this summer, and got better with every match here. But I have improved my game as well. Venus was hitting her powerful shots with much more consistency, which makes her much more dangerous. She is someone I will have to watch."

Williams told reporters, "You could not have a better champion than Martina. She's an all-around player. She's consistent and has a lot of shots. She's had a great year."

It wasn't over yet. In the fall, Martina captured two more singles titles and three more doubles titles. The 1997 season had been more than great—it had been phenomenal! In one year, Martina had won 12 singles titles and 8 doubles titles. She achieved the No. 1 ranking in March and kept it all year. The WTA Tour unanimously voted her Player of the Year. *Tennis* magazine also named her as their choice for that honor. They also named Melanie Molitor Coach of the Year in recognition of the tremendous support and encouragement she had given her daughter. The world couldn't wait to see what Martina would accomplish next.

CITIZEN

6

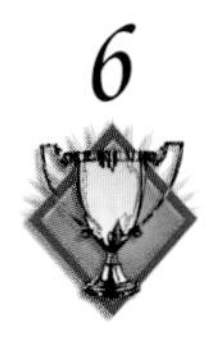

Growing Pains

It was the question on every tennis fan's mind: could Martina Hingis continue her incredible winning streak? She had missed winning a Grand Slam by only one match at the French Open in 1997. Maybe 1998 would be the year.

Martina's appearance at her first tournament of the year in Sydney surprised everyone. She had gained weight and looked out of shape; she also seemed moody and irritable. In the second round, Martina was upset by Venus Williams, a player she had beaten many times before.

Coach Melanie Molitor, however, sounded philosophical about her daughter's loss. "A new year always brings different challenges," she said. "Last year Martina struggled with a knee injury after falling off a horse. This year it will be something else. Maybe it's the age she is. It is up to me to find new ways to get her through it and to play her best tennis."

At the Australian Open, Martina faced some stiff competition from players like Anke Huber, Mary Pierce, Conchita Martinez, and Anna Kournikova. Somehow Martina found the strength and determination to hang on.

Fans pack the U.S. Open stadium for the 1999 women's final between Martina Hingis and Serena Williams. The 1998 and 1999 seasons tested Martina in many ways, but she responded with increased maturity and enthusiasm.

"I said after the first week that if I wanted to stay in the tournament I had to improve. That's what I did. With each match, I got better and better. After I lost in Sydney, I practiced more and everything paid off."

When the tournament ended, Martina owned both the singles and the doubles trophies once again. That year, she became both the youngest player in the Open Era to defend a Grand Slam title and the youngest player to earn more than $5 million in prize money in one year.

Martina didn't have much time to celebrate. Only one day later, she began defending her title in Tokyo. She played well enough to reach the final but lost to an American player, Lindsay Davenport. Martina's next opportunity to win came in March at Indian Wells, California. Throughout the tournament, she competed intensely and won her matches in a dramatic way. Martina avenged her loss to Davenport in Japan by beating her in straight sets at Indian Wells.

Said Martina, "[N]o one can beat me when I'm playing my best tennis. Some of the girls are stronger and taller than I am, but I'm just a little bit smarter than them all. I wish I was 5' 9" so I could have a big serve like Mary Pierce, but I'm not. So I just have to be smarter and win the big points. Now that I'm in better physical shape, it will be very difficult for anyone to beat me." When people remarked that this 17-year-old's comments sounded a little arrogant, Martina responded, "I am number one in the world, so I have the right to be arrogant!"

In spite of her confidence, Martina had more challenges and distractions than she could handle in 1998. She had trouble focusing on her game. She struggled with the emotional ups and downs that all teenagers go through as they become adults. At the Lipton Championships, reporters observed that Martina seemed to be a lot more excited about walking around the tournament site with her new boyfriend than she was about competing on the court. She lost to Venus Williams again, this time in the semifinals.

In Germany, Martina came back to defeat Jana Novotna for her third title of the year. For most players, three titles in one year is an impressive accomplishment. But by that time the previous year, she had won twice as many.

At the Italian Open, Martina triumphed over several new teenage sensations, including Mirjana Lucic and Anna Kournikova. She had to face Venus Williams in the final. The widely anticipated rivalry finally became a reality. This time, Martina was ready to play. She avenged her loss at the Lipton by beating Williams 6-3, 2-6, 6-3.

Although Martina won the trophy, she lost the spotlight. Venus Williams and her younger sister Serena stole the show. They caused quite a commotion when they met in the quarterfinals of the Open. As the newspaper headlines said, "Martina Hingis Wins the Title, but Sisters Williams Win the Crowd."

A journalist had once asked tennis champion Billie Jean King what dangers she saw ahead for young Martina Hingis. King replied, "She has no history yet. She *is* only 16. She doesn't have any memories of choking or losing to an unranked player. It will happen. A bad patch happens to everyone. How will she handle herself?"

In 1998, after more than three terrific years on the tour, 17-year-old Martina finally hit her first bad patch. After the Italian Open, Martina failed to win another singles title for six months.

She appeared sluggish and disinterested on the court. She made unusual errors and unnecessary mistakes. Martina skipped practices and workouts to concentrate more on her social life. Her lack of focus showed in her results. She lost in the semifinals at both the French Open and Wimbledon.

When Martina failed to defend her titles, Lindsay Davenport won them. When Martina struggled to get to the final of the U.S. Open, Davenport was there waiting for her. Davenport not only took the title but also took away Martina's No. 1 ranking.

For Martina, 1998 turned out to be a very disappointing year. The one bright spot of the season was her doubles performance. After winning the title in Australia, she went on to capture the doubles titles at the French Open, Wimbledon, and the U.S. Open—winning the doubles Grand Slam.

Coming into the Chase Championships, the last tournament of the year, Martina desperately wanted a victory to end her six-month title drought. She put serious effort into her performance and regained her focus. One match at a time, she worked her way through to the final and a showdown with the new No. 1 player in the world, Lindsay Davenport. Once again, Martina's hard work and determination paid off. She beat Davenport 7-5, 6-4, 4-6, 6-2.

"Today I just felt much better," Martina expressed. "I was running better and I hit harder. I made some great shots, but you have to do that against Lindsay. If you don't, you are out of there!" She added, "It's a good feeling to have going into next year. I am very happy about this title." As the No. 2 player in the world, Martina looked for a fresh start in 1999.

She couldn't wait to play in Australia, where she had experienced so much success. "I always do well in Australia," Martina said. "This is my . . . territory!"

She wasn't disappointed. At the beginning of '99, Martina defeated French teenager Amelie Mauresmo to win the singles title. With her victory in the doubles, Martina became the only player (male or female) in history to win the same Grand Slam tournament in both singles and doubles for three consecutive years.

However, Martina made headlines for more than her on-court success. She found herself in the center of a major controversy. During a press conference, Martina had made some unflattering comments about her opponent, Amelie Mauresmo. Some things may have been blown out of proportion or taken out of context, but her remarks made sports headlines all over the world. Instead of clarifying what she had said or apologizing for her words, Martina made the mistake of denying that she had ever said them. The sports journalists then announced that they had her comments on tape. Because of her response, Martina came across as both mean-spirited and dishonest. She had no idea how her careless words would come back to haunt her later on.

In Tokyo, Martina won her second straight title and, more importantly, regained the No. 1 ranking. Her results over the next few months were mixed. Sometimes she won, sometimes she lost. In April she defeated Anna Kournikova for the trophy at Hilton Head, South Carolina. The next month, Martina won the German Open without dropping a set. She wasn't dominating as she had in 1997, but she kept coming back.

The French Open was the only Grand Slam

Martina has learned to face reporters with confidence rather than arrogance. She is now able to discuss learning from her mistakes and looks forward to facing the challenges her career will bring.

title Martina had yet to win. She went into the tournament with high hopes. But the 1999 event proved to be one of the most difficult experiences of her life.

Although many people had completely written off tennis great Steffi Graf, she had come back from numerous injuries to play on the WTA Tour for one last season. Graf shocked and inspired the tennis world with her run to the final, showing flashes of brilliance from her glory days. The crowd cheered loudly for their sentimental favorite, while actively rooting against Martina. People had grown tired of Martina's cockiness and her put-downs of other players. They hadn't forgotten her unkind remarks about their countrywoman Amelie Mauresmo.

Martina got some bad calls during the match. She argued with the linespeople and the chair umpire. In her frustration, she began banging her racquet around. Then she made what one sportswriter called a "monumental mistake in judgment." She violated tennis etiquette by crossing to her opponent's side of the net to argue a call. The chair umpire assessed Martina a point penalty for unsportsmanlike conduct. She would later be fined $1,500 by the ITF. It just gave the hostile crowd more reason to jeer her.

After a grueling two hours and 25 minutes, Steffi Graf closed out the match and added the crowning touch to her magnificent career. It was Graf's sixth French Open title and the 22nd Grand Slam title of her career.

When the match ended, Martina ran off crying uncontrollably. The crowd booed her off the court. She would not have come back for the trophy ceremony if it hadn't been for her mother's insistence. Arm-in-arm, mother and daughter walked back onto the court together. Tears were streaming down Martina's face, but somehow she managed to give a gracious speech and accept the runner-up trophy.

Humiliated by her defeat, Martina wanted to make some changes. She decided she needed more independence. She began to argue more with her mother about her practices and social life. Then, in the summer, Martina traveled to Wimbledon by herself, leaving her mother behind. After losing dismally in the first round, Martina realized she had made a mistake. She still needed her mother's love, support, and advice. Melanie Molitor and Martina patched things up. Together they tried to find Martina' s winning form once again.

It's been said that the true test of a champion is not how many titles and awards he or she achieves, but how he or she handles adversity. Throughout Martina's career, she had been watched closely. The tennis world wanted to see if she had the true character of a champion. The 1998–1999 seasons tested Martina as she had never been tested before in her career.

"I had an open road," Martina admitted. "I don't think I understood really what was going [on] there at that time. I kept winning, but I didn't really appreciate it because it was just so easy."

Now if she wanted to succeed, she would have to work hard. Martina did find her way back in 1999. She won three more tournaments—in San Diego, California, Canada, and Filderstadt—for a total of seven singles trophies and four doubles titles. She reached the finals of the U.S. Open once again, losing a tough match to tennis's hottest new player, Serena Williams, Venus Williams's little sister.

In her interviews, Martina showed newfound maturity. She still had plenty of confidence and attitude, but she talked a lot about learning from her mistakes, working hard, and looking to the future.

In her six years on the professional tour, Martina Hingis has shown the growth and maturity that come from experience. At 20 years old, her career is far from over. She may yet enter the history books as the greatest tennis player of all time.

Statistics

Year	Date	Career Singles Titles	Ranking
1993	October 24	Langenthal (ITF Futures)	—
1996	October 14	Filderstadt (Germany)	10
	November 11	Oakland	6
1997	January 11	Sydney (Australia)	4
	January 26	Australian Open	2
	February 2	Tokyo (Pan Pacific)	2
	February 16	Paris Indoors (France)	2
	March 29	Lipton Championships	1
	April 6	Hilton Head	1
	July 6	Wimbledon	1
	July 27	Stanford	1
	August 3	San Diego	1
	September 7	U.S. Open	1
	October 12	Filderstadt	1
	November 16	Philadelphia	1
1998	January 31	Australian Open	1
	March 15	Indian Wells	1
	May 3	Hamburg (Germany)	1
	May 10	Italian Open	1
	November 22	Chase Championships	2
1999	January 31	Australian Open	2
	February 7	Tokyo (Pan Pacific)	1
	April 4	Hilton Head	1
	May 16	German Open	1
	August 8	San Diego	1
	August 22	Du Maurier Open	1
	October 10	Filderstadt	1

Chronology

1980	Born on September 30 in Kosice, Slovakia (then Czechoslovakia)
1991	Wins first international junior title, the European Championships
1994	Captures junior titles at the French Open and Wimbledon; named ITF Junior Player of the Year; turns professional on October 14, just days after her 14th birthday
1995	Becomes youngest female player in the Open Era to win a singles match at the Australian Open; reaches No. 16 in the professional rankings; named WTA Newcomer of the Year
1996	Wins first WTA Tour professional singles title at Filderstadt, Germany; wins second title in Oakland; cracks the Top 10 in the rankings; named WTA Most Improved Player
1997	Captures three of the four Grand Slam events of the year—the Australian Open, Wimbledon, and the U.S. Open; becomes the youngest player ever to reach No. 1 in the world rankings on March 31
1998	Earns over $3 million in prize money for the second straight year; wins the Australian Open and the season-ending Chase Championships; captures doubles Grand Slam
1999	Becomes the only player in history to win the singles and doubles titles in the same Grand Slam event (the Australian Open) for three consecutive years; captures fifth Grand Slam title

Further Reading

Mewshaw, Michael. *Ladies of the Court: Grace and Disgrace on the Women's Tennis Tour.* New York: Crown Publishers, 1993.

Rambeck, Richard. *Martina Hingis, Sports Superstar.* Plymouth, MN: Children's World, 1998.

Sanchez-Vicario, Aranxta. *The Young Tennis Player.* New York: D.K. Publishing, 1996.

Schwabacher, Martin. *Superstars of Women's Tennis.* Philadelphia: Chelsea House Publishers, 1997.

Spencer, Bev. *Martina Hingis.* Toronto: Warwick Publishing, 1999.

Teitelbaum, Michael. *Grand Slam Stars: Martina Hingis and Venus Williams.* San Francisco: HarperCollins Juvenile Books, 1998.

About the Author

A former elementary school teacher, CHRISTIN DITCHFIELD is now a full-time writer, author, and conference speaker. Her interviews with celebrity athletes have appeared in magazines all over the world. Ms. Ditchfield makes her home in Sarasota, Florida.

HANNAH STORM, NBC Sports play-by-play announcer, reporter, and studio host, made her debut in 1992 at Wimbledon during the All England Tennis Championships. Shortly thereafter, she was paired with Jim Lampley to cohost the *Olympic Show* for the 1992 Olympic Games in Barcelona. Later that year, Storm was named cohost of *Notre Dame Saturday*, NBC's college football pregame show. Adding to her repertoire, Storm became a reporter for the 1994 Major League All-Star Game and the pregame host for the 1995, 1997, and 1999 World Series. Storm's success as host of *NBA Showtime* during the 1997-98 season won her the role as studio host for the inaugural season of the Women's National Basketball Association in 1998.

In 1996, Storm was selected as NBC's host for the Summer Olympics in Atlanta, and she has been named as host for both the 2000 Summer Olympics in Sydney and the 2002 Winter Olympics in Salt Lake City. Storm received a Gracie Allen Award for Outstanding Personal Achievement, which was presented by the American Women in Radio and Television Foundation (AWRTF), for her coverage of the 1999 NBA Finals and 1999 World Series. She has been married to NBC Sports broadcaster Dan Hicks since 1994. They have two daughters.

Photo Credits:
Rusty Kennedy/AP/Wide World Photos: 2; Steve Holland/AP/Wide World Photos: 8, 13; New Millennium Images: 10, 17, 49; Trevor Collens/AP/Wide World Photos: 14; Chris Gardner/AP/Wide World Photos: 20; Lionel Cironneau/AP/Wide World Photos: 23, 40; Stuart Ramson/AP/Wide World Photos: 26; Kathy Willens/AP/Wide World Photos: 30; Adam Butler/AP/Wide World Photos: 35; Giulio Broglio/AP/Wide World Photos: 36; Dave Caulkin/AP/Wide World Photos: 43; Elise Amendola/AP/Wide World Photos: 50; Roberto Borea/AP/Wide World Photos: 52; Larry Marano/London Features, Int'l: 58.

INDEX